KT-227-290

THE
COLLECTOR'S
CORNER

WATCHES

Order No:
Class: 739.3 WAT
Accession No: 066607
Type: L

THE LEARNING CENTRE
TOWER HAMLETS COLLEGE
POPLAR CENTRE
POPLAR HIGH STREET
LONDON E14 0AF

WATCHES

Grange BOOKS

A Quantum Book

Published by Grange Books
an imprint of Grange Books Plc
The Grange
Kingsnorth Industrial Estate
Hoo, nr Rochester
Kent ME3 9ND

Copyright © 1999 Quantum Books Ltd

All rights reserved.
This book is protected by copyright. No part of it may be reproduced, stored in a retrieval
system, or transmitted in any form or by any means, without the prior permission in
writing of the Publisher, nor be otherwise circulated in any form of binding or cover other
than that in which it is published and without a similar condition
including this condition being imposed on the subsequent publisher.

ISBN 1 84013-292-2

This book is produced by
Quantum Books Ltd
6 Blundell Street
London N7 9BH

Project Manager: Rebecca Kingsley
Art Director: Siân Keogh
Project Editor: Jo Wells
Designer: Sandra Marques
Editor: Linda Doeser

The material in this publication previously appeared in *Wristwatches* and
Wristwatches A Connoisseur's Guide

QUMCCWT
Set in Gill Sans
Reproduced in Singapore by Eray Scan Pte Ltd
Printed in Singapore by Star Standard Industries (Pte) Ltd

CONTENTS

COUNTING THE HOURS AND WATCHING THE MINUTES

• • • •

RIGHT The time-
telling obelisk,
Cleopatra's
Needle, once
stood outside the
temple at
Heliopolis in
Ancient Egypt.

The only basis for measuring time in ancient days was the rotation of the Earth, and the apparent path of the sun from east to west across the sky was used by the first astronomers to divide the days and nights into regular units.

Early timepieces

When humans ceased to be nomadic hunters and began to settle into communities, they felt the need to split the day into something less vague than sunrise, noon and sunset. Having noticed the differences in the length of shadows cast by the sun, they erected sticks, and later taller constructions, the shadows of which could be measured and related to the passage of time.

Some of these pillars were used to mark periods of the year – the Great Pyramid in Egypt, designed in part to determine the equinoxes, is an early example. So, too, is the great circle of Stonehenge in England, which was erected around 1900 B.C. It is thought that, in the past, on Midsummer's Day, the sun rose over the heelstone at the time of the summer solstice.

Time-sticks and sundials

Somewhere around 1000 B.C. came the time-sticks of Egypt. These were T-shaped pieces of wood with raised crosspieces which cast a shadow on the long shaft. The shaft was engraved to mark regular periods of time – the first 'hours'. It was placed facing east in the morning and had to be reversed to face west in the afternoon.

The time-stick was the forerunner of the sundial, which is also believed to have originated in Egypt. To begin with, a vertical bar, called a gnomon, cast a shadow on a horizontal dial. Later, the stick-like gnomon was replaced by an angled one pointing north and inclined according to the place of origin. The time could then be told not

LEFT England's Salisbury cathedral boasts a particularly fine example of an ancient clock.

by the length of the shadow, but by its direction on the dial, a far more accurate process.

Water clocks

Another early device for measuring the passing hours was the clepsydra, or water-clock. It is said to have originated in China, where several different forms were developed, and was certainly used in Babylon around 1500 B.C. An early type found in the Temple of Amon

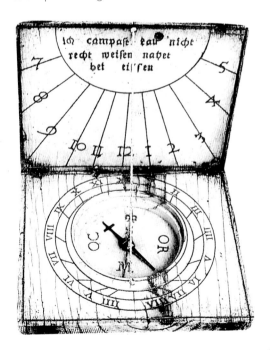

LEFT Pocket sundials were one of the earliest portable timepieces and were probably invented in Egypt.

7

*RIGHT The entire
purpose of the
ancient Egyptian
pyramids remains
a mystery, but one
of their uses was
to mark the
equinoxes.*

at Karnak in Egypt consisted of an alabaster bowl with rings and inscriptions on the outside and a small hole near the base. As the water ran out through the hole, the falling level could be made to show the hours. The outflow hole consisted of a drilled gemstone set into the alabaster. In this, it was a little like the jewelled bearing in a modern wristwatch.

Portable clocks

Although water-clocks were not particularly handy objects, it took several centuries for their successor to be developed. Sand- or hour-glasses first appeared in the thirteenth century. An early illustration shows two glass bulbs bound together at the necks with a pierced diaphragm designed to restrict the flow of sand from the upper to the lower bulb. By measuring out the sand, the time taken for it to flow from the top to the bottom could be controlled. Sand-glasses were relatively easy to make, they were portable and they were fundamentally more accurate than water-clocks.

Sand-glasses were the industrial timers of the earliest factories. They were invaluable at sea, too, where, suspended from the ceiling, they operated well, even when the waves were rough. They were also a common sight on the pulpits in churches, measuring the length of the Sunday sermon. But they were counters – they did not actually tell the time.

LEFT Watches in this early twentieth-century production line were made entirely by young women, probably because their fingers were nimble and their eyes were sharp.

Inventing the wristwatch

Long before production lines came into existence, a cottage industry existed in Switzerland, France and Germany, where poor farmers, after trying to make a living from infertile soil during the summer months, would spend long winter days and evenings producing, cog by cog, the forerunners of today's wristwatches.

Although the first portable timepiece was said to have been worn by Marie Antoinette in the eighteenth century, the first true wristwatch was not invented for another hundred years. Patek Phillipe is thought to have made the first wristwatch in 1868, but some say that a Brazilian named Alberto Santos-Dumont, who was conducting experiments with an 'airship', mentioned to

his friend, watchmaker Louis-François Cartier, how inconvenient it was to pull out his pocket watch while he was at the controls of his flying machine. When Santos-Dumont completed his record-breaking 220-m (240-yd) flight in 1907, he was wearing the first Cartier Santos-Dumont on his wrist.

Since then, few collectables have also been as useful in everyday life as the wristwatch, even though it has only one purpose – to measure the passing of time. Wristwatches have become available for all occasions, ages and types of people. They are made of materials as diverse as plastic and precious gold, some incorporate works of art, while others have novelty faces. There is, indeed, a design to suit everyone.

ABOVE This early, delicate lady's watch by Cartier is attractively coloured, proving that this is not just a modern fashion.

ABOVE LEFT Although modern, this Dunhill watch is based on a traditional design.

RIGHT Swatch
watches have
been collected
virtually since they
were first
produced. This
1990 Swatch
Chronograph sold-
out immediately it
was introduced.

Collecting watches

The aim of this book is not to tell you what to collect, but rather to help you decide for yourself by showing you the variety of watches available. A watch collection can be based around any number of features, such as

RIGHT Le Crash,
this extraordinary
watch by Cartier
is considered a
classic by
collectors.

the date of production, the materials used or the particular functions of the watch. A collection can also be based on a theme, such as military or sports watches. The following pages will help you decide which way you want your collection to grow.

Whatever type of watch you choose to collect, you would be well advised to start with pieces that you like and find interesting. A purchase that is based on price or rarity alone may eventually be regretted.

A wristwatch collection has one advantage over most others in that you can actually wear it every day, swapping your watch to match your mood, your clothes or the occasion. By reading, observing and visiting museums, shops and salerooms you will gradually acquire greater knowledge. Once you have started to learn about watches, the process will continue naturally until you can rely on your experience and instinct to be your guides. With growing confidence in your own judgement, you will be able to look further afield, daring to buy a piece that is a little bit special and learning to trust your developing 'feel' for what is good.

CHAPTER ONE

TELLING THE TIME

• • • •

In 1511 a young German locksmith named Peter Henlein built the first really portable personal timekeeper using a small coiled spring – much as he used in his locks – and a scaled-down train of gears. They called it the 'Nuremburg Egg'. This timekeeper, now called a 'watch', inspired craftsmen all over Europe, especially in Geneva, where a flood of French and German refugees, many of whom were watch- and clockmakers, had fled from religious persecution. Watchmaking quickly became one of Switzerland's most important industries.

Early watchmakers

Some early watches were wound by a key through the one hand (clocks with two hands had been in existence for only about 25 years) and had a bow at 12 o'clock through which a ribbon or chain was threaded so that they could be hung around the neck.

In 1675, Christian Huygens, who had invented the pendulum clock, introduced the spiral hairspring, which made for greater accuracy and allowed the introduction of a minute hand on watches. It was about the same time, that men began wearing waistcoats. What was more natural than to slip a watch into a pocket instead of hanging it around the neck?

BELOW The Armorial Bearings of the Worshipful Company of Clockmakers.

RIGHT Abraham-Louis Breguet, watchmaker and inventor.

The next hundred years was the golden age of clock- and watchmaking in England, with some of the greatest ever watchmakers working there. Thomas Mudge (1715–1794) had been working on an idea for an anchor escapement for watches that was similar to the one used in pendulum clocks. In 1759, he made a watch with a lever escapement. This was arguably the most important invention in watchmaking after the balance spring.

This was followed by another far-reaching development. Until then, the pivots of the train had run in metal bearings, causing wear and resulting in loss of accuracy. A Swiss living in England thought of using a ruby as a bearing, both at the end of the pivots, and pierced as a bearing in the plate. The English not only took up this technique with enthusiasm, but they kept it to themselves. It vastly improved the smooth running of watches and their accuracy.

Swiss supremacy

Switzerland, too, had its innovative watchmakers. Foremost among them was Abraham-Louis Breguet (1747–1823), whose contributions to watchmaking include the self-winding watch – first invented by Abraham-Louis Perrelet around 1770 – a shock-protection system and the tourbillon, a device to offset the effects of gravity. From the 1770s to the end of the nineteenth, pocket watches became increasingly sophisticated.

This period also saw the founding of some of Switzerland's great houses, headed by Vacheron Constantin in 1755, Blancpain, Jaeger-LeCoultre, Longines, Cartier and IWC, who belonged to an elite band of manufacturers who made every part of their watches, including the movements, themselves.

RIGHT Grande Complications combine telling time with every known function – perpetual calendars, moonphases, stop/start mechanisms, alarms, repeaters, strikes and even thermometers..

Watches became increasingly complicated, incorporating repeaters, phases of the moon, perpetual calendars and chronographs, but they still tended to be bulky, as their movements were protected by double cases (known as 'hunters') with a hinged cover over the glass.

Watch movements

Today there are three basic watch movements: hand-wound, automatic and quartz. The first two are both called mechanical. It is important to know which is which, as a hand-wound watch will not start when shaken, but most automatics will start when wound.

Mechanical watches

The hand-wound wristwatch is the direct descendant of the key-wound pocket watch, which, in the course of its evolution, acquired a winder or, as it is more properly known, a crown and stem. First recorded in 1770, the automatic movement also has quite a long history. The pedometer movement was first mentioned in 1780.

A watch with an automatic movement is wound when the wearer moves around, causing a weighted segment or rotor to pivot on itself.

An Englishman, John Harwood, was responsible for the first automatic wristwatch. He began experimenting in London in 1917 and applied for a Swiss patent in 1923. The wristwatch he perfected was unusual, even by today's standards, as it did not have a crown. It had to be set by turning the bezel (the metal frame holding the watch glass) and it had to be shaken to be wound. Previously, wristwatches were hand-wound. Harwood wristwatches were manufactured in Switzerland until the early 1930s, when the company went bankrupt.

Electro-mechanical watches

The advent of miniature batteries designed for hearing aids in the 1950s inspired a French company, LIP, and an American manufacturer, Hamilton, to join forces for research purposes. As a result, the first electric wristwatches became available in 1957. They were large, ugly and not very popular with one exception, the Accutron. Created by a Swiss electronics engineer and with an accuracy of 99.9977 per cent, it was issued by Bulova with the first-ever guarantee of accuracy for a wristwatch. Before Bulova was able to elaborate on the idea, the public's interest waned and the concept of the electro-mechanical wristwatch was abandoned.

LEFT The plate bearing the manufacturer's name, Zenith, is the rotor which provides the power to the mainspring in this automatic movement..

ABOVE This Hamilton battery-operated Electric from the 1950s is highly collectable.

13

RIGHT These tiny Omega movements could never have been produced without quartz technology.

BELOW The movement of this 1960s Longines automatic Conquest is unusual in that it has a power reserve indicator in the centre of the dial.

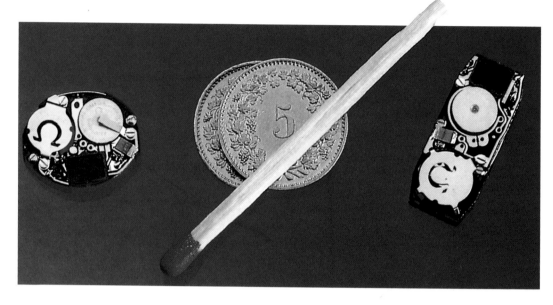

The first quartz wristwatch

Quartz clocks had existed for some time before quartz watches. During the 1960s, electronics engineers in Japan and Switzerland were working towards the first quartz wristwatch and finally, in 1968, both countries had prototypes. These proved to have a remarkably small margin of error – only two seconds per day. Unfortunately, as with their predecessor, the electro-mechanical wristwatch, they were ugly and clumsy in design.

Manufacturers began to feel that telling the time with a dial and hands should be superseded by something more in keeping with the watch's revolutionary movement. Liquid crystal displays (LCDs) and light-emitting diodes (LEDs) were extensively used. It soon became apparent that both methods had disadvantages linked to their display. This, plus the fact that such watches could be produced very cheaply in the Far East, soon moved the LCD and the LED production out of traditional watchmaking areas and both jewellers and watch shops decided that the end-product was not of good enough quality.

Innovation and tradition

The Swiss watch houses went back to the centuries-old tradition of dial-and-hand display. This, coupled with quartz technology, has resulted in some of the most outstanding-looking timepieces of today. It is now possible to produce ultra-thin, elegant wristwatches. These pieces, when fitted with a mechanical movement, were and still are in a very high price bracket.

Movements in common

All watch movements work on the same principle. The time divider, which divides passing time into equal parts, must receive power. There must be a system for transmitting power from the source to the divider. Finally, the watch must show the time after the divider has completed its task – either on a dial or on a digital display.

The mainspring of a mechanical watch is tightened either by the turning of the crown on a hand-wound watch or by the swinging action of the rotor for an automatic. Any watch movement should be treated with the respect that the care of its manufacture warrants.

Other components

Three materials are traditionally used for the crystal or glass dial cover: plexiglass, quartz crystal and synthetic sapphire. The third of these is the most expensive to produce and is used only on higher-quality pieces or watches made to withstand

LEFT The watch cases of the Tissot Rock Watch range, launched in 1985, are made of mother-of-pearl.

rough sports usage. It is scratch-resistant, but nothing is totally scratch-proof and it can still break! Older sports watches tend to have a plexiglass crystal. Quartz mineral crystal, which is somewhere between plexiglass and sapphire crystal in strength, is used on many 'everyday' watches.

Materials

Apart from any precious stones on a watch case or bracelet, the list of watchmakers' materials is as long as it is varied. Gold has been used in fine pieces since the beginning. The most versatile of metals, it is used in both heavy sports watches and tiny cocktail pieces. Surface scratches can be polished out; precious stones may be set into it; its colour can be changed by adding other metals; and its value may be higher or lower according to the carat weight. The finish can be enamelled over, left highly polished or be brushed over.

Rolled gold was used widely until the 1960s, when gold plating became a better proposition. Rolled gold is made by placing a

LEFT This Rolex dress watch from the 1930s is made from 9-carat gold and has a gold bracelet.

BELOW The 1955 Omega Sapphette takes its name from its faceted sapphire watch crystal

15

RIGHT This Midi
size Rolex Oyster
from the 1940s is
made of stainless
steel.

FAR RIGHT Jaeger-
LeCoultre's gold
Memovox, first
made during the
1950s, was such a
successful design
that it was still
selling in the
1960s.

BELOW The
'bootlace' strap of
this Cartier lady's
watch is typical of
the 1920s.

layer of base metal between two thin layers of gold and running the 'sandwich' between rollers. Gold plate is made by putting base metal into an acid bath in which gold particles are suspended and passing an electric current through. It is not always easy to tell the two apart, although gold plate generally has a slightly 'harder' shine when it is polished.

Silver has also been employed in the manufacture of wristwatches, but not so extensively as stainless steel. This is the material most often used for sports watches, with or without gold or gold plating. It is virtually unalterable and it is possible to find quite early wristwatches made of steel which show remarkably few signs of wear.

Other materials used in more modern pieces include several organic materials, such as pieces of rock, slabs of shell and even wood. The wide choice of man-made materials includes ceramics, tungsten carbide, strontium titanite, fibreglass and plastic. In

particular, the Rado watch company, has experimented with these new materials and the resulting pieces are outstanding in design and durability, combining both style and strength.

Straps and bracelets

When a wristwatch is made, a strap or bracelet is incorporated into the design. Choosing which depends on how the watch is going to be used. Earlier pieces usually had leather straps, with extensions for wearing over sportswear, but metal bracelets soon followed because they were more durable or more stylish.

A fine gold bracelet emphasized the elegance of the watch itself. Some lady's watches had ribbon straps, but very few of these models retain the original strap.

If the metal bracelet is the original, it will be made of the same material or combination as the watch case. It will probably be stamped with the manufacturer's name or logo. If a leather strap is used, check the buckle: if it is the original, it will have some identifying marks on it. It is very important to look over the strap or bracelet when buying a vintage wristwatch, mainly from the point of view of safety. If the strap or bracelet has deteriorated beyond repair or is absent, try to replace it with one as close as possible to the original. Sometimes, the manufacturer may be able to assist you.

CHAPTER TWO

FROM THE RIDICULOUS
TO THE SUBLIME

• • • •

It was mainly American manufacturers that first made wristwatches available to ordinary people. Around 1850, a group of watch companies got together with the idea of making a watch for the masses. The plan was to make thousands of identical interchangeable parts which could be assembled by cheap labour. After several false starts, the Waterbury Clock Company produced a watch that sold for $3.50. Their ambition was to get the price down to $1.00.

The first man to do so was Robert Ingersoll who, with his brother Charles, ran a mail-order business. Every item in their catalogue sold for $1.00. Ingersoll persuaded the Waterbury Clock Company to make him a small clock movement by giving them an order – quite large in those days – for 12,000 units. He housed them in a case he designed himself.

His first models, with a chain, sold for $1.50. They were so successful that, two years later, he went back to Waterbury with an order for half a million pieces; he sold them for $1.00. He had achieved his ambition to sell a watch for a day's pay, and christened his product 'The watch that made the dollar famous'.

By the early 1900s, the line included a lady's model, called the Midget. When the demand came for cheap wristwatches for the armed forces, it was simplicity itself to solder a pair of wire lugs at 12 and 6 o'clock and run a strap across the back. The world's first cheap wristwatch was born! It still had the

LEFT Mail-order businessman, Robert Ingersoll sold his watches for a day's pay.

BELOW The watch that made the dollar famous.

ABOVE The world's first inexpensive wristwatch.

crown on top, but when that was later moved to 3 o'clock, it looked much the same as its more expensive counterpart.

Ingersoll's other innovation was to devise a form of luminous paint that was applied to hands and numerals so that the troops could see the time in the dark. He called his invention Radiolite. Using radium compounds, which are radioactive, to make luminous paint has subsequently been banned on health grounds.

Swiss adaptations

The idea of using machinery to make accurate and interchangeable parts was not confined to cheap watches. Many prestigious Swiss companies took to the idea and improved the quantity and extent of their output without jeopardizing quality because the parts were still assembled by hand. English watchmakers, however, declined to have anything to do with these ideas from America and so the watch industry in England went into a decline from which it has never recovered.

The Swiss realized that the secret lay in the quality of the machine tools used. Many firms already employed engineers of the highest calibre. Georges-August Lechot, for instance, had designed and built a range of machines for Vacheron Constantin that revolutionized

the firm's production as far back as 1843. Nevertheless, because the majority of Swiss watches at that time were of the better-quality jewelled-lever variety, they were still relatively expensive.

Mass production

American companies were not the only ones to have considered the possibility of making a cheap watch for the masses. In the middle of the nineteenth century, a German watchmaker named Georges-Frédéric Roskopf working in La Chaux de Fonds decided he could make a watch for 20 francs. He set about simplifying the

RIGHT The official certificate of 'Chronometer' quality.

escapement, eliminating a number of parts and replacing the jewels in the lever by pins. He modified the winding and cheapened the case. Much to the surprise of the industry, he received a bronze medal at the Paris Exhibition of 1868. A century later, the Swiss were exporting 28 million 'Roskopf' watches a year and were the world's leading suppliers of cheap watches.

Traditional watchmakers did not think much of Roskopf's watches to start with – initially, many were poorly made – but as production became more refined, pin-lever watches achieved a quality that was quite respectable in relation to their price. One Swiss manufacturer, Oris, entered pin-lever watches in an official trial and was awarded a certificate of 'Chronometer' quality, much to the disappointment of the jewelled-lever fraternity.

By the 1960s, the watch industry in the middle and upper price ranges was more or less dominated by the Swiss and they could be forgiven for thinking that the watch had reached its zenith. Firms, such as Audemars Piguet, IWC, and Patek Philippe were creating complicated timepieces with multiple functions, hand-finished to an incredible degree of accuracy and housed in fabulous engraved and bejewelled 18-carat gold cases. What more could anyone want?

Interesting movements

The function of watches is to tell the time. However, they may do many other things which can be used as the focus for a collection. Whether quartz or automatic, a complicated movement only adds to the intrinsic value of a watch, as well as looking attractive. Fashions

come and go in the watchmaking industry, as they do in more or less any other business. During the late 1980s, for example, the public was crying out for moonphase wristwatches, although it had not actually realized that they had been around for a number of years in a variety of different forms. As a result, older wristwatches with moonphases and other complicated movements fetched record prices in the international salerooms.

The collector's primary concern should be the beauty of the wristwatch itself, plus, perhaps, the hours of labour that have gone into creating it and the dedication of watchmakers whose thirst for knowledge made them look deeper into the possibilities of their craft. Such watches are not necessarily prohibitively expensive, for with care and research, it is possible to find interesting pieces at quite reasonable prices. This part of the chapter is designed to help you recognize what you are looking at, so that you are not simply staring at a watch face and seeing a mass of hands and dials without having any idea of their function.

When you have bought a watch with a complicated movement, handle the mechanism with care, especially when no instructions are available. Do not attempt to adjust it or set the various displays until you are absolutely sure that you know what you are doing. If necessary, find an expert and ask for explanations.

*ABOVE
Rectangular moonphases, such as this one from Jaeger-LeCoultre, dating from 1949 are comparatively rare.*

RIGHT This world timer was made by Patek Phillipe.

International time

With the increase in travel for both business and pleasure, it has become more important to have a watch on which the different time zones can be seen at a glance. This is especially true for the business person who works with communications networks spanning the world. The principle of the time zone movement is quite simple. A rotating disc or interior bezel is marked with the name of a major city from each of the 24 time zones and an extra set of hands or another dial will track the time of the chosen zone.

For a long time there have been watches capable of giving the time in two different time zones and even keeping track of two different dates. In the case of quartz movements, all these functions are spectacular in themselves. For an automatic movement, the difficulty lies in fitting in the extra bezels or dials, plus the additional set of hands, together with a date window or dial, without making the watch very awkward to operate and, at the same time, keeping the buttons and winders to a minimum. The finer the manufacture, the thinner the movement will be. After all, these are not necessarily sports watches and a degree of elegance is required.

Power reserve

The *réserve de marche*, or power reserve, is a feature found on some automatic wristwatches. It is sometimes paired with another feature, such as a world timer, but quite frequently exists by itself. The power reserve indicates how many hours the watch will run if left untouched. It is generally shown by a single hand running over a scale numbered either from 1 to 36 or from 1 to 48, depending on the type of movement.

Repeaters

A minute repeat movement is the only one which tells the time by sound and it first appeared in wristwatches at the beginning of the twentieth century. At the push of a button, the watch can be set to strike the hours, quarter-hours and minutes. This is made possible by a complex mechanical memory, created by a combination of the watchmaker's art with that of the metallurgist, whose skills are needed for the manufacture of the hammers and gongs. There have to be at least two different tones available in order to tell the hours and

quarter-hours apart, for instance. The idea behind this type of movement is simple. Before the advent of luminous paint, it was not possible to tell the time in the dark, so another method had to be found – consequently, the minute repeater was invented.

A pioneering company in this field was Audemars Piguet, which claims to have produced the smallest minute repeater movement in the world. The company is also unusual in that it produces a rectangular minute repeater, which certainly adds to the collectability value.

Alarms

As with the minute repeater, the problems of making an alarm wristwatch with an automatic movement are not just to do with watchmaking, but also metallurgic. Unlike in a quartz movement, where an electronic sound can easily be produced, there must be metal striking metal to produce a sound.

One of the most famous alarm wristwatches is surely the Grand Reveil by Jaeger-LeCoultre. A most interesting feature is the alloy used for its gong, which dates

LEFT This contemporary world timer from Ebel is self-winding and has a 40-hour power reserve.

BELOW The simplicity of Blancpain's 18-carat, yellow gold repeater conceals a very sophisticated movement.

21

RIGHT The
Memovox by
Jaeger Le-Coultre
has an automatic
alarm system.

A contemporary automatic alarm watch made by Maurice Lacroix, which combines a good sound with good looks, is worth looking out for because of the scarcity value of mechanical alarm wristwatches.

The moonphase

The moonphase indicator on a watch dial can turn the banal into the special. Some of the movements linked to the indicator can be quite simple, merely showing a rotating moon which can be set more or less accurately. Others will take into account the lunar month, showing the twenty-nine and a half days with the various phases of the moon positioned accordingly.

Until recently, Cartier produced a moonphase movement (quartz) for its Santos range, which, unusually, was available as a lady's or a man's model. It is comparatively rare to find a moonphase indicator on its own; it is frequently linked with a date display.

Calendars

A proper calendar movement does not just indicate the date. In general, it comprises day and date, month and, perhaps, a moonphase. A quartz calendar movement will normally be

RIGHT This
Cartier watch
combines
chronograph,
moonphase and
calendar.

back to the Chinese Bronze Age when it was well known for producing a clear and pure sound. This gong is separated from the movement so that its vibrations will not have a detrimental effect. For Jaeger-LeCoultre, the Grand Reveil was the culmination of many years' experience of manufacturing mechanical alarm wristwatches. Another of the company's famous products was the Memovox wristwatch, made during the 1950s, which was, in fact, the first automatic wristwatch to feature an alarm function.

Perpetual calendars

The first perpetual calendars are thought to have appeared around 1853. A perpetual calendar movement takes up where the ordinary calendar movement leaves off. It should not require any adjustment for leap years, thanks to a complicated system of wheels and satellite wheels or bearings, generally linked to the month display. In most cases, the watch's calendar display will not need to be touched until the year 2100 when, because of Pope Gregory XII's reform of our calendar in 1582 (whereby the year consists of 365 days and a leap year occurs when the year's number is divisible by four), either a minor adjustment will be needed or a small part will have to be changed.

LEFT A Cartier watch combines calendar, moonphase, and chronograph.

BELOW The Cosmic, dating from 1947, was the first Omega calendar watch that indicated the exact time – day, date and month – and moonphase.

programmed to take into account the different lengths of the months. However, an automatic one will not be, unless it is a perpetual (a self-winding automatic) movement. It is important to ensure that the displays for the day, date and month are correctly synchronized; if they are not, the information will be incorrect.

The information is displayed by one of three methods: dial, windows or a combination of both. There are no set rules about the position of each of these, so when buying a calendar watch, simply look for one that you find legible and think looks nice. Some people maintain that the more dials there are on a watch face, the more difficult it is to absorb the information at a glance. This may well be true of watches where the design and final appearance have not been properly thought through and tested at the planning stage. However, with increasing experience, it will not take long before you are able to differentiate between a good dial design and a bad one that provides confusing information or, worse, misleads the eye.

RIGHT This modern quartz chronograph by Dunhill includes a calendar movement.

BELOW Blancpain's understated contemporary quantième perpétuel is made from 18-carat gold.

Quantième perpétuel

The feature known as *quantième perpétuel*, which is often linked to a calendar or perpetual calendar function, indicates the ability of the watch to adjust itself to the specific, but changing number of days in each month: 28, 29, 30 or 31. Again, the term can be applied only to mechanical watches. It is possible to have this function only if there is some kind of mechanical memory built into the watch's movement.

Grande Complication

Only attempted by few manufacturers, the *grande complication* is a combination of minute repeat, chronograph and perpetual calendar. A piece with this kind of movement is a collector's item even before it leaves the drawing board and is the direct result of centuries of Swiss watchmaking tradition.

Although the case will certainly be made of the most precious of metals, this is one of the few instances where the movement is infinitely more valuable than the case. *Grandes Complications* first appeared in the nineteenth century and all seem to have originated in the Swiss Vallée de Joux, near Geneva. The first wristwatch versions were produced only in the late 1980s.

COLLECTING

● ● ● ●

The first thing to do when starting a collection – of watches or anything else, for that matter – is to find out as much as you can about the subject. There are masses of both popular and scholarly books on the subject of watches. Catalogues from the famous auction houses, such as Christies, Phillips, Sothebys and Antiquorum in Geneva, are valuable sources of information about what is available and at what price. They can, however, be expensive to buy.

Visiting auction rooms is also often extremely useful, even if you are not actually planning to buy anything. At specialist auctions, there will be lots of watches on display, and the saleroom staff are usually most helpful. If at all possible, go to previews, when there is plenty of time to browse, and then to the auction as well to allow you to compare estimates with the actual prices paid. It will also help you get a better feel for the market and to estimate the accuracy of your own judgement.

LEFT A free poster was on offer for every Ingersoll watch sold, ranging in price from the Yankee at $1.00 to the Triumph at $1.75. Both the watches and the poster are now collector's items.

RIGHT A device designed to block the outer bezel to allow for accurate adjustment of the time makes these Longines watches interesting.

The next thing to decide is exactly what you are going to collect. There are hundreds of different types of watches: men's, women's, pocket, wrist, plain, complicated, sports, dress and so on. It helps to concentrate your sights on a small area to begin with – you can always enlarge it. If you extend your choice too far at first, you may find yourself trying to sell off unwanted items before you have really got started.

You may also find it helpful to study up-to-date specialist magazines. Some are purely trade journals and will give you useful information about current models. Others are available only to members of particular societies. There are also magazines aimed at collectors which contain articles on auctions and prices and give background information about famous brands.

BELOW In 1933, Mickey Mouse appeared for the first time on a watch..

It will also pay to study the history of watches in general. Particular dates are important – the launch of the first wristwatch, for example – since they provide a reference point on which to base your own collection. Early quartz models from the 1970s might be an interesting area to explore. The first Swatches, for example, are now fetching high prices.

Try to be original. If your chosen type of watch is too easy to come by, your collection will not be very special. That is why collectors go for limited editions from the great manufacturers – they know that the model is exclusive right from the start.

Museums and collections

There are collections of watches in one form or another in most major towns, where both public museums and private collections are excellent sources of information. Many countries, including the United States, France, Germany and Great Britain, have contributed to make the watch industry one of the most fascinating and changing and there are tangible records of this across the world.

Many watch manufacturers have their own private collections which may be visited by appointment. The Longines headquarters at St Imier in Switzerland, for example, has its own museum, which houses some pieces of historical importance and goes right back to the origins of the brand.

Buying

Most towns have jewellery shops which sell both old and new wristwatches. Do not hesitate to ask if they have anything else apart from the goods displayed. Untold treasures have been dug out of dusty boxes lying dormant at the back of stockrooms.

One of the best places to buy is your local auction room. Auctions these days are well-regulated affairs with well-trained and, for the most part, friendly approachable staff, who are only too glad to offer help and answer questions. Equally, if you go to one of the major salerooms in a large city, they will even be able to tell you what will be going on sale in all their branches, even those on the other side of the world.

It is important to keep an open mind when bidding for a particular watch. Do not forget that you may not be the only person interested in it. Never stay in the bidding for longer than you mean to, just because the price looks as if it will be only slightly higher than you plan to pay. Local taxes and auction house charges (generally between 10 and 15 per cent) are added on top of the price reached in the bidding. Keep this in mind to avoid unpleasant shocks when it finally comes to paying for your purchase.

Part-exchange

One way of keeping your collection 'alive' is to buy with part-exchange. If you feel that a watch does not belong in your collection, put it aside for part-exchange. When you spot another piece that you feel does belong, take your old watch along and see whether the seller will lower the price of the watch you want in exchange. This always works best when you are 'trading up'.

BELOW Keep your eyes open in shops and salerooms. This pretty little bangle has an early Rotary watch concealed inside.

WRISTWATCH CHRONOLOGY

19TH CENTURY

1838
Louis Audemars invents stem winding and setting mechanism

1868

Patek Philippe makes the first wristwatch

1871
Aaros Dennison of the International Watch Company (IWC) invents the waterproof watch case

1880
Girard-Perregaux produces a wristwatch for officers of the Imperial Austrian Navy

1888

Cartier produces a lady's wristwatch with diamonds and gold bracelet

1900–09

1902

The first Omega wristwatch is produced

1902
93,000 wristwatches sold in Germany

1903
Louis Brandt, founder of Omega, dies

1904
One of the most famous early wristwatches appears – the Santos-Dumont, produced by the House of Cartier

1910–19

Auguste Agassiz

1910
Longines begins wristwatch production

1911
Santos-Dumont wristwatch goes on general sale

1912
Movado makes an army wristwatch with a protective grid over the glass

1914
The first alarm wristwatch is made by Eterna

1917
British Royal Flying Corps issued with wristwatches made by Omega

1918
Omega supplies US Army with wristwatches

1920–29

1920

Audemars Piguet produces the smallest repeater watch – 16mm (⅝in)

1923
Invention of the automatic wristwatch by John Harwood (the prototype is made by Blancpain)

1925
Patek Philippe produces the first wristwatch with a perpetual calendar

1927
First water-resistant Rolex Oyster produced

1930–39

1930
The smallest lady's watch movement to date – baguette shaped – is produced

1930
Tissot develops the first anti-magnetic wristwatch

1932
Launch of Reverso by Jaeger-LeCoultre

Manufacture of the Lindbergh Aviator by Longines (to the design of Charles Lindbergh)

1933
First watch for children made by Ingersoll (featuring Disney's Mickey Mouse)

Longines made official time-keeper at the Brazilian Grand Prix

1936
Omega appointed official timekeeper for the Olympic Games

1940–49	1950–59	1960–69	1970–79	1980–89

1940–49

Hamilton supplies US forces with wristwatches; Omega and Breitling supply RAF watches during the war years

1945
Rolex Date/just is the first watch with a date display on the watch face

1946
Audemars Piguet produce the thinnest wristwatch in the world – 1.64mm (⅟₁₆in)

American Nathan George Horwitt designs the Movado Museum Watch

1950–59

Poljot, the first Russian wristwatch, is produced – later to become Sekonda

Tissot develops Tissot Navigator, a self-winding wristwatch with a universal calendar

Rolex Submariner goes down 305m (1,000ft)

1952
Breitling introduces the Navitimer, a super chronograph designed especially for pilots

1953
Lip's battery-powered watch is introduced

1957

Hamilton produces the first electric watch

1960–69

1960
Bulova launches Accutron, the electronic tuning-fork watch invented by Max Hetzel

1966
Girard-Perregaux produces the first high-frequency mechanical watch (36,000 vibrations per hour)

Creation of Beta 1, the first Swiss quartz movement

1969
Girard-Perregaux develops the first mass-produced quartz watch

International Watch Company introduces the Da Vinci wristwatch

Longines produces the first quartz cybernetic wristwatch

Zenith brings back the El Primero, the epitome of chronograph movements

Neil Armstrong wears an Omega Speedmaster Professional on the moon

1970–79

1972
First stainless-steel luxury wristwatch is made (Audemars Piguet)

1972
Longines launches an LCD (liquid crystal display) watch

1975

Launch of Raymond Weil brand, with innovative ultra-slim movement

1976
Launch of Maurice Lacroix brand

1978
Vacheron Constantin Kallista is sold for US$5,000,000

1980–89

1983

Swatch is launched

Rolex Sea Dweller goes down to 1,220m (4,000ft)

Longines launches the Conquest range, accurate to about one minute in five years

1985

Tag-Heuer brand appears on the market

1986
Tissot brings out the Rock Watch

1987
Tissot introduces the TwoTimer (a watch showing both analogue and digital display)

Hints and tips

Once you have decided what to buy and where to buy it, there are a few points to bear in mind when purchasing a vintage wristwatch. If you are going to wear the watch, it needs to be capable of telling the time. If it is not, it requires repairing to return it to working order. With a quartz watch, this may be a simple matter of replacing the battery, but bear in mind that a service and overhaul may add quite a lot of money to your overall outlay in purchasing a watch.

If a mechanical wristwatch is not in working order, there could be any number of of reasons. If a ticking sound can be heard when the watch has been wound, but the hands are not moving, it is possible that they have come away from the dial train (the wheels and pinions of a watch). Not all wristwatches, especially early ones, were made to be shock-resistant and the hands may have become disconnected after a severe knock. This is not a major problem and can usually be put right by a competent watch repairer.

However, if there is complete silence, the watch cannot be wound or there is a 'grinding' feel when you try to wind it, the problem could be more serious and, again, the possible repair costs must be taken into account when you are considering purchasing the watch.

RIGHT Limited editions are often scrupulously logged at the manufacturer's headquarters.

LEFT Limited edition watches are almost always individually numbered. This piece is number 15 out of a total production of 300.

Limited and special editions

Whether buying old or new, beware of the difference between a limited and a special edition. With a limited edition, only a relatively few watches are produced and each will carry a number that is individual to it. A special edition may be a commemorative piece or a production tied to some sporting event. There will be no set number but there may be a note about the commemoration on the back.

Caring for your collection

Mount your collection of wristwatches on rolls of soft fabric or acid-free tissue paper, if the watches do not have their own boxes.

Never leave dead batteries in quartz watches. If a mechanical wristwatch stops, get it serviced straight away. Find a reliable watch repairer early in your collecting career and stay with him or her – as a bonus, you will also learn a lot.

Your collection will occasionally need cleaning. This means the outside only. Never clean, oil or regulate the movement or change the battery yourself. Always leave the inside of a watch to the professional repairer. A soft cloth is all that is needed to clean the case of most metal watches. Never use solvents on gold plate or silver gilt. Silver watches may be rubbed gently with impregnated cloth. The metal part of a waterproof watch may be cleaned in soapy water and then dried.

Documentation

When you buy a new watch, you should be issued with the appropriate box, a valid guarantee, a full set of instructions matching the movement of the watch (unless the operation of the watch is so basic that you do not need instructions) and, most important of all if the watch has the word 'chronometer' on the dial, a certificate proving that it has passed stringent testing.

When buying a second-hand item, remember that the rarer and more valuable it is, the more documentation will add to its value. The original guarantee, stamped by the first retailer, together with the right box, can add a great deal of money to the asking price.

RIGHT Even by 1990's standards, Jaeger LeCoultre's 1930s Duoplan is outstandingly accurate.

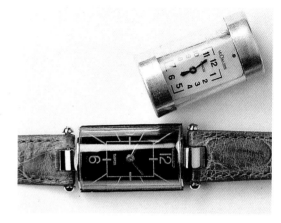

Buyer beware

Before buying, thoroughly examine the watch with a magnifying eyeglass. Do not forget to check the strap or bracelet as well. If you are buying the watch to wear, it will not stay on your wrist for long if the pins (lugs) are bent or the stitching on a leather strap is worn.

Although several grades of leather are used for straps (the most water-resistant being sharkskin), you are not likely to find the original leather on a vintage watch. The finer the watch, the better the grade of leather the original strap would have been. Whether boarskin, ostrich skin, calf, crocodile or lizard, if you wet a leather strap regularly, it will deteriorate quicker, and the harder you intend to wear the watch, the stronger the strap needs to be. In fact, if you are going to wear it frequently for sports, a metal bracelet is best; otherwise resign yourself to buying a new leather strap fairly often.

BELOW Promoted as 'conceived for sportsmen, sailors and colonials' the Omega sports model is now showing signs of its age.

One problem with metal bracelets that you should look out for is stretching. If the links seem very far apart with large gaps between them and a lot of 'play', the bracelet needs professional attention. If it is made of gold, the metal may have become worn and the lugs inside the links may also be worn or distorted.

A watch with a machine-made gold bracelet will be less expensive than one with a mainly hand-assembled, loose-link type. The problem likely to occur after a number of years is splitting: this can be repaired by a competent goldsmith, but the repair always shows and the split may recur in a different position.

Organizing your collection

Each piece in your collection should have its own file containing a photograph, the date and place of purchase, any important serial and model numbers and information regarding related pieces. This file should also contain any guarantees or chronometer certificates issued by the watch manufacturer.

OMEGA

L'heure exacte pour la vie

Montre "MARINE"
ÉTANCHE A L'EAU ET A LA POUSSIÈRE

Staybrite inoxyd. Fr. **800** SPÉCIALEMENT CONÇUE POUR SPORTIFS, MARINS ET COLONIAUX

CHAPTER FOUR

DECADES OF DESIGN

• • • •

Outside influences have touched watch design just as they have affected everything. With experience, it is possible to date a piece just by glancing at it, as it reflects the style of its time.

Because early designs were often linked to wars or sports, they tended to have a heavier look to them, reflecting the style of the pocket watch from which they were direct descendants. As the technology was mastered and then perfected, movements could be made for finer and finer cases. Finally the dainty, elegant lady's pieces became feasible.

Twenties

After the quiet elegance of the Edwardian era came the 'Roaring Twenties' and Cubism. Its influence was felt throughout the home, spreading into the sphere of personal adornment and accessories – and watches were no exception. The style was meant to reflect the new liberalism and leave behind the stifled ideas of the previous age. The concept that a utilitarian object could be good to look at was implanted in people's minds and would influence the design of everyday wristwatches. Handsome pieces would no longer be reserved for the privileged, as their price was gradually being made more accessible, thanks to the advances of mechanization on the early assembly lines.

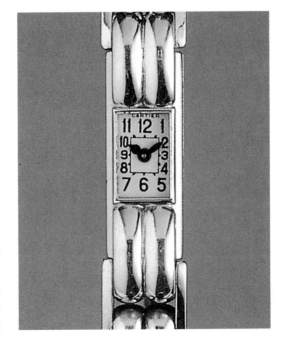

LEFT This 1928 gold lady's watch is typically elegant, with a small movement and a slim bracelet.

Rendez-vous de chasse et de sport
vous imposent une LONGINES

Advertising that dates from this era shows that manufacturers were promoting the idea of a different watch for each activity or aspect of the wearer's life – one for sports, one for formal occasions and one for casual and office wear. This was probably because the techniques required to make the more delicate-looking watches strong enough to withstand tough sports wear were simply not available at that time and the cases for the more elegant styles could not take the pressures of vigorous physical activity.

Thirties

ABOVE AND RIGHT Advertisements for Longine watches in the 1930s promoted the idea of 'lifestyle' watches.

The 1930s signalled the end of Prohibition and a new fluidity to the old structures of the previous decade. Surrealism was now the buzz word and, at the same time, the man or woman on the street began to show an interest in sporting activities. Watches for golf, such as the Reverso by Jaeger-LeCoultre, date from the beginning of the 1930s. Whereas men's watches were becoming more masculine in looks to complement the new outdoor lifestyle, watches for ladies' evening wear were growing smaller and more delicate in design, reflecting the new fashions.

Pour vos courses, au printemps,
prenez une LONGINES

34

Forties

During World War II all the efforts of manufacturers were directed towards supplying the combat forces, and civilians were generally expected to make do with utility goods or with pre-war products. As a result, there are very few watches, other than military ones, from the period. A few attractive jewellery pieces still exist. Their small size is an indication of how difficult it was to find the materials needed for their manufacture. Some watch companies actually stopped making timepieces during the war years, supplying small machinery parts to various government agencies instead. Any new designs were usually plain and unornamented, and on straps rather than on metal bracelets.

ABOVE The original models of the Jaeger-Le Coultre Reverso (1932) were mechanical.

Fifties

After the years of austerity materials became more readily available. As the blue-collar class in both Great Britain and the United States grew in size, designers were setting their stamp on everything, from table lamps to motor cars. Couturier Christian Dior's 'New Look' was an ode to extravagance after the lean years. Watch design gradually regained its momentum and became more adventurous.

LEFT The red-tipped hands on both these Jaeger-LeCoultre calendar watches from the 1940s indicate the date.

BELOW There is always an exception – the 1945 Jaeger-LeCoultre Mysterieuse. The small single diamond is the minute indicator and the larger one indicates the hours

However, there was still a lack of unnecessary frills, and designs were generally sober and clean-cut. Watches had unadorned bezels, plain hands and straightforward functional dials. Lady's watches still tended to be very small and neat, with boot-lace straps or the ubiquitous 'elasticated' metal bracelet. Although there was an emerging youth market, hungry for consumer goods, increasingly fashion-conscious and influenced by Hollywood stars, such as James Dean, watch manufacturers continued to concentrate on the established section of the population. The case design remained nothing more

ART WATCHES

ABOVE *The enamel dial of this 1952 Longines art watch depicts an astral theme.*

RIGHT *A painting by Roy Lichtenstein inspired the design of this Jean Lassale watch.*

The fine line between art and watch design was crossed in the late 1940s by the American artist George Horowitz. His watch design, famous for its simplicity and still available, features a plain black dial with a single gold dot marking twelve o'clock. Since then, several watch companies have maintained a tradition of asking an artist to design a piece or to allow one of his/her works of art to be incorporated into one of their creations.

For several years, the Movado watch company has commissioned watches from major artists. One who made an impact was the late Andy Warhol, with his Times/5 wristwatch. With five different photographs of New York as individual dials, this piece has five separate watch movements. It was a limited edition of 250; 50 pieces were retained by Movado and 200 went on sale in 1988 for $18,500 each.

Movado also invited Yaakov Agam to design for it. In 1989, he produced the Rainbow collection which

included not just a wristwatch, but also other timepieces presented in four separate sets. These reflected the artist's interest in sculptural works.

His achievement was followed in 1990 by The Color of Time, created by Arman, a neo-realist painter and sculptor. Presented in a maple-wood box, which he also

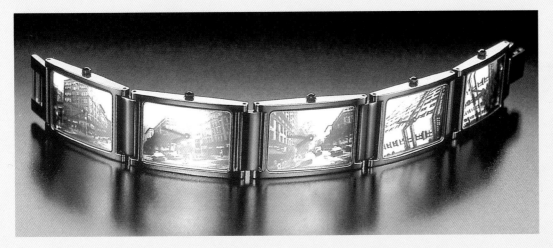

LEFT Andy Warhol died before the completion of Times/5, adapted from his design by Movado in 1988

designed, these wristwatches have paint brushes instead of hands and swatches of colour instead of numerals. The theme is also carried over to the watch strap.

In 1991 James Rosenquist presented Elapse, Eclipse, Ellipse – three watches with mechanical movements, made of silver and with a dark blue leather strap decorated with silver stars. Ellipse represents the Earth as seen from outer space, Eclipse represents a meteor and Elapse is an abstract concept of time. The piece is packaged in a pyramid-shaped box.

Another design from Movado is its new art watch by Max Bill, called Bill-Time and produced as a limited edition of 99 pieces. The colour patterns on the dial and bracelet are inlaid under tiny sapphire-glass plates.

Movado is not the only company that bridges the gap between art and design. The Jean Lassale company was responsible for the creation of a watch based on a 1962 painting by Roy Lichtenstein. It has an 18-carat white gold dial, engraved with the painting's golf-ball motif. Other more accessible watches include Omega's Art watches or even its Symbol range, which features mystic signs on the watch dial.

BELOW The box is an integral part of James Rosenquist's concept for Elapse, Eclipse, Ellipse.

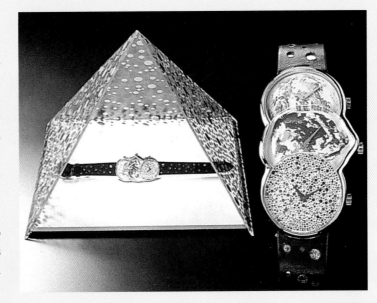

than a shell for the mysterious workings inside. Equally, this may just have been a reflection of the starkness creeping in from the world of household interiors, where the use of new synthetic materials was leading to a total revolution in style.

Watches were still seen as functional items, except perhaps by the leading names, with little or no fashion appeal to the young. The watch as a fashion statement for those from six to sixty was still a long way off, not least because the average cost of a wristwatch was then quite high compared to average earnings.

Sixties

ABOVE In the late 1940s and early 1950s, only the big watch companies showed any interest in more unusual designs.

As the 1960s progressed, the high-profile brands took a more daring approach. Op Art reached its peak at this time and something of its concept inevitably filtered down to such functional objects as the watch.

Every design concept of the 1960s, in the watch world at least, seemed to be 'sturdy'. Gone were the delicate little lady's watches of previous decades. As the watch market found its feet within the maze of new technological advancement and the public grew more discerning, fresh ideas were welcomed. A profusion of colours was used in

both lady's and men's jewellery watches: turquoise, coral and amethyst all featured. Piaget produced some outstanding watches during the decade that are displayed in museums today.

It was also at this time that Omega produced the classic Dynamic. Although not a jewellery watch, its design was typical of the period. First produced in

ABOVE This 1958 Omega advertisement presages the extremes in design that would follow in the next decade.

LEFT The stylized dial of this Cartier man's strap watch is dates unmistakably from the 1960s

LEFT Rado's Diastar 48, issued in 1973, demonstrates the company's interest in unusual case materials.

the late 1960s, with a thick oval case and a very wide strap, it was made to be durable. A production run of over one million means that the Dynamic design can still be seen today and the straps continue to be made – proof of an enduring design.

Seventies

The progressive style of watch design in the late 1960s and the 1970s may have been owing to the fact that Swiss watch manufacturers were having to compete against a wave of inexpensive Far Eastern digital watches flooding the market. Technological excellence was not enough; the product had to look good as well to compete in an increasingly crowded marketplace.

The 1960s had been a decade of contrasts, with burgeoning consumerism on the one hand and growing environmental awareness on the other, so it is not surprising that the watch industry started to lose its

direction. This contributed to the upheavals of the 1970s, when the coming of quartz led to a revolution in the trade and extremes in design.

The youth culture of the late 1970s and early 1980s and the advent of the 'yuppie' culture created increasing demand for good-quality fashionable watches. The Swiss watchmaking industry showed new confidence by making more fashion-conscious pieces at prices formerly reserved for conservative lines. Designer watches started to appear to satisfy a label-hungry public, and fashion houses, such as Christian Dior, Yves St Laurent and Gucci, had watches designed to complete their 'look' for the season. These pieces were generally made

BELOW This Cartier lady's gold watch on a leather strap reflects the changes in both art and design of the 1970s.

RIGHT The power
dressing business
woman of the
1980s required a
smart, chic watch,
such as this
Rodolphe piece
with its highly
individual dial.

with gold-plated cases and Swiss watch movements. Such watches can make an interesting collection: the colours and materials may be slightly more adventurous than those used by the true watch houses.

Eighties

With the 1980s came the 'statements'. Fashion trends were arriving thick and fast and people had the money to keep up with all the changes. To show off these marvellous new clothes and accessories and to impress on the boss that you were raring to go, you had to be fit, so you had to participate in a sport – and needed a sports watch. The industry was quick to cater for this, and it was soon hard to find a brand that did not possess a sports range.

BELOW The
watch case and
bracelet are
perfectly
integrated in this
stylish 1990s
Rado wristwatch.

However, to match their versatile lifestyles, people still wanted slim, elegant dress pieces. The mid-1980s saw the emergence of some highly-stylized pieces with strange shapes. For instance, the Sectora, by Jean d'Eve, had unusual hand movements dictated by the shape of the case. There was also a considerable growth in small watch companies, cashing in on a fad for retrospective pieces using good-quality Swiss quartz movements in old-style shaped cases. Michel Herbelin and Emerich Meerson both made very attractive watches with sound movements and some may still be found today.

Nineties

Sports watches maintained their popularity in the early 1990s, but there was an increase in models falling into the middle ground between sports and dress – and some sports pieces even showed a few diamonds. The interest in reviving old designs had not died out and copies of earlier watches remained popular, either as true replicas or by taking the original design as the basis for a new version.

RIGHT A 1990 limited edition art
watch by Movado, called The Color of
Time was designed by Arman.

SPORTS WATCHES

• • • •

There are specialized watches for many kinds of sport, including diving, flying and yachting. These sports watches probably have one thing in common – their size. Sports watches tend to be slightly larger and heavier than watches for day-to-day wear because of the higher degree of water and shock resistancy that is often required by the sportsperson. Extra space is often needed to incorporate the extra movements demanded from a sports watch.

Many sports watches have a ratchet bezel, which enables the specific timing of, for example, a dive or a run. On all good watches, this bezel is unidirectional so that, in the case of a blow to the watch in which the bezel is moved, diving or flying time, say, is shortened, not prolonged. If you purchase an old sports watch to use for a potentially dangerous sport, it is essential to check the overall condition of the piece, making sure that the stated water resistancy is still maintained and that the ratchet bezel is intact.

Water-resistant watches should have their seals checked regularly, especially if they are used in salt water, which corrodes the inner sealing ring. There are many water-resistant chronograph movements, but the chronograph cannot be activated or de-activated under water.

ABOVE The Porsche designed Ocean 2000 by the International Watch Company is water resistant to a depth of 2000m (6,560ft).

LEFT Two handsome gold sports watches by Raymond Weil.

Baume et Mercier is one such firm. Its Transpacific and Riviera ranges, both available in steel, mixed metal and 18-carat gold, are fully water-resistant to at least 30m (100ft) and they are equipped with sapphire glass. The Riviera range has a chronograph among its many models and the Transpacific is a chronograph range which, unusually, contains a lady's model.

Continuing the Baume et Mercier history of chronograph ranges, many of the company's 1950s models are still to be found today and these also show the same elegant looks.

Baume et Mercier

ABOVE The attractive Breitling Navitimer (left) with another classic: the Breitling Automatic Chronograph (right) from the Chronomat range.

As many watch companies have proved, sports watches do not all have to be ugly and awkward. There is often no distinction between the functional and the beautiful. Sports watches can have surprising good looks but maintain the ability to withstand normal sports wear. These are available today, both as current lines and as past successes.

Breitling

Breitling is well known for its specialist sports watches. Many older models are still in existence, some of which have links with important aviation events and air forces all over the world. Breitling is no stranger to the chronograph movement, and perhaps its most famous in recent years, the Chronomat, is available in many guises. This automatic chronograph has a diving bezel and is water-resistant. Breitling also produces the Cosmonaute, a watch for the pilot, which has a slide-rule bezel and a 24-hour movement.

RIGHT This drawing of the Breitling Chronomat demonstrates the slide rule feature of this watch.

ABOVE Titanium is the metal used for the Breitling Aerospace – standard issue to the RAF Red Arrows.

The company supplies many aviation organizations, and its flagship chronograph, the Navitimer, is still produced by the factory in Grenchen, Switzerland.

Their precision and the ease with which crucial information is made legible are probably the main reasons why Breitling timing instruments have claimed a very important position on the instrument panel of many a legendary aircraft, such as the Boeing Clipper and the DC3. You can often see retired employees wearing their official-issue Breitling.

The yachtsman is also catered for with the Breitling Yachtmaster, which has an automatic chronograph movement and five-and ten-minute warning zones.

ABOVE. Two Girard-Perregaux watches, one in steel and one in 18-carat gold.

Cartier

In view of the growing interest in sports watches, it is not surprising that such a great name as Cartier should unveil its Pasha range in 1985, named after El Glaoui, Pasha of Marrakesh, who in the 1930s requested a watch that he could wear in his swimming pool. The Pasha is one of Cartier's most distinctive ranges, available in either steel or 18-carat gold. Cartier has also fitted a revolutionary movement to one of the Pasha series, the Chrono Reflex. This is not just a chronograph, but also a calendar watch, and its case seems amazingly small when the number of functions is taken into consideration. The Chrono Reflex has an ingenious system for indicating the number of years to go until a leap year, as well as the date, the month and the hour according to the 24-hour clock.

Girard-Perregaux

Girard-Perregaux has applied its many years of experience to the production of both classic and sports chronographs and also offers a range of diving watches, called Sea Hawk, which would satisfy the most exacting collector. The classic good looks of its GP 4900, one of few watches

LEFT. The Diablo is a 1990s Cartier sports watch fitted with the chrono-reflex movement.

MILITARY WRISTWATCHES

Collecting military wristwatches has many devotees. Experience can be gained by talking to members of the forces or consulting watch companies' literature. Books are rare. Hands-on experience is important.

Military wristwatches have interesting technological features and historical connections which can be used as the basis for a collection. Some enthusiasts collect only World War II infantry wristwatches, for example.

LEFT This pilot's wristwatch, made by IWC in 1940 was designed to be worn over a flying suit.

RIGHT Omega produced wristwatches for the US military, made during WWI.

Military wristwatches first appeared during World War I, when it was discovered that it is difficult to shoot while trying to check the time on a pocket watch. They seem to bear plenty of clues as to their provenance, but few direct pointers.

Generally speaking, a pilot's wristwatch will have a centre second hand, while an infantryman's or ordinary foot soldier's watch may have a second hand dial above the six on the watch face. Wristwatches designed for use by pilots also tend to be a little larger than other military watches, so that they can be strapped to the leg and used as navigational tools when needed.

BELOW From top to bottom: a World War I half hunter in solid silver; A World War I silver Zenith Land and Sea c1916 and a Hamilton wristwatch c1944–50 made for the US and British armed forces.

Marking on the case backs of military wristwatches will give a clue as to whom they were issued and for what purpose. '6B' may be found on pieces issued to the British RAF and to the crews of aircraft carriers; 'W10' on British land army watches. American watches are often marked with a US Army patent and the name of the corps or division. WWW on cases stands for waterproof wristwatch. Military wristwatches often came with a webbed canvas strap and had black dials.

During World War II in the United States, the products of the Hamilton watch company played an important part in naval operations. A special undersea Hamilton watch was designed and made specially for the underwater demolition teams. When working with delayed timers on explosives, precision timing was critical, so these wristwatches played a significant role and probably saved many lives.

You may come across the World War I term 'hack watches'. One of the jobs of a plane's navigator was to give his crew a time check so that they could synchronize their watches and this was known as 'hacking'. These 'hacks' were often Hamilton wristwatches.

Many military wristwatches were and still are produced by some of the big watch companies, such as IWC, Omega and Jaeger-LeCoultre (in very rare instances); others are produced by companies specializing in military supplies. Military wristwatch production is not confined to wartime: contemporary pieces find their way into shops and auctions and their provenance is easier to verify.

Not all the names found on military wristwatches will be familiar – names such as Smiths, which produced watches for the RAF, CWC, which made both quartz and mechanical wristwatches, and Vertex. All these are well known for their military productions and are ideal for the novice. Make sure that you are buying a genuine military wristwatch and not just a souvenir piece.

ABOVE From top to bottom: British Pilot or Aircrew watch, by Omega, with Air Ministry markings; 1969 Smiths wristwatch for the British Army; 1987 CWC British service issue wristwatch with a Swiss movement.

RIGHT Longines
Conquest
chronograph series
was produced to
commemorate the
Munich Olympic
Games in 1972

BELOW The
Omega
Speedmaster
Professional was
chosen by NASA
in 1965 for use on
space missions.

available in pink gold, are reminiscent of an earlier age, while the company's commitment to the future is demonstrated in the clean, sober lines of its GP7000 series. In production since 1990, again using both yellow and pink gold, GP 7000 is a range of true sports watches with sapphire glass and automatic movements.

Longines

Since 1867, when Ernest Françillon opened the Longines factory, the company's name has been linked to major sporting events, with the commitment to precision timing that this entails. It manufacturers marine chronometers needing to withstand the rigours of journeys to the Arctic and the Antarctic (not the least famous of these expeditions was led by Captain Bernier, when he navigated from the United States to the North Pole on his ship, *The Arctic*). As well as producing watches for sports from motor racing to cycling, Longines has been directly involved in great sporting events throughout the twentieth century.

Omega

Omega's Speedmaster chronographs also have a long history. A hand-wound version was taken to the moon in 1969 – you can't have an automatic movement in the absence of gravity. With such an auspicious start, it is not surprising that Omega has kept up the Speedmaster range, retaining the basic idea, but constantly improving and updating the design. Introducing a titanium and rose gold Seamaster has been Omega's latest venture into chronographs, with a water-resistancy of 300m (1,000ft) and a ratchet diving bezel. It is worth knowing that Omega first went underwater in 1934, so it is not surprising that the company has solved the problem of helium gas release in a novel way. Instead of having an open valve, it has perfected a screw-down crown at ten o'clock, which can be opened if needed, letting out any helium, while preventing water from seeping in.

Omega in space

When the Omega Speedmaster went to the moon, it was the beginning of a great tradition in sports timing for the company. Omega has produced a limited-edition Speedmaster chronograph with a run of just 999 pieces and available only in 18-carat gold. The survivor of a very impressive array of tests organized by NASA in Houston, Omega beat its competitors and, after that first moon mission, accompanied the US astronauts on several more sorties. An agreement between the Russians and Omega followed.

ABOVE Omega's 1934 pilot's watch has a revolving bezel with an arrow index for measuring flight duration.

Commemorating twenty years of excellence

To commemorate the twentieth anniversary of that important date of 20 July, 1969, Omega also produced an edition of 2,500 stainless-steel Speedmaster professional chronographs, each inscribed, as is the more recent 18-carat gold version, with the words 'Apollo XI 1969' on the edge and bearing on the back 'The first watch worn on the moon' and 'Flight qualified by NASA for all manned space missions'.

It is worth remembering that the precision of these chronographs was so good that it enabled the crew of one space mission to make crucial calculations to establish their position when contact with Earth was broken.

ABOVE A 1933 advertisement for Omega sports watches.

LEFT The contemporary Rolex Submariner is water resistant to 300m (1000ft)

RIGHT In the early 1990s Zenith produced The Rainbow containing the El Primero movement.

Rolex

One of the most famous diving watches of all time must surely be the Rolex Submariner, with an automatic movement, chronometer certificate and water resistance to 300m (1,000ft). It is beaten only by another Rolex product, the Sea Dweller. It is capable of submerging to a depth of 1,220m (4,000ft). This is the only Rolex with a date that does not have a magnifying bubble. The Sea Dweller has been produced solely in steel, whereas the Submariner has been produced in steel, yellow metal and steel, and 18-carat gold.

Tag-Heuer

BELOW A Tag-Heuer Formula 1 Chronograph.

It would be impossible to collect sports watches and ignore Tag-Heuer. Tracing its history back to 1860 and official timekeeper at the 1920 Olympics, Tag-Heuer has made a remarkable comeback since the early 1980s. In 1985, the link between the watch Heuer and the group TAG (Techniques d'Avant Garde) was made. Any piece with only the Heuer name pre-dates 1985.

Most of the Tag-Heuers of today have a quartz mechanism, ensuring precision. Edward Heuer's interest in technological achieve-ment led to many patents, the first, early in the company's history, being for a new system of water-sealing cases. In 1942, it launched the Solunar, which showed the ebb and flow of the tides and indicated the times when fishing would be good! The company's expertise has also been used to make car dashboard timers.

Today the Tag-Heuer factory is still in a position to service most wristwatches bearing the old Heuer brand name, be they mechanical or quartz. Automatic Tag-Heuers are rare and much sought after.

Zenith

It would be difficult to discuss automatic chronograph movements without mentioning the El Primero movement by Zenith, used by other watch companies for their chronograph ranges. The El Primero is a classic, constantly revised and updated. It was first produced in 1969 and has been making a considerable comeback recently. It is thought by some watch enthusiasts to be the epitome of chronograph movements, having, as it does, many unique features. Zenith has recently produced a new range of El Primero chronographs, entitled The Rainbow.

CHAPTER SIX

JEWELLERY

• • • •

A watch should suit the personality and lifestyle of the wearer. For some people a watch is a purely functional object, to others it is an important piece of jewellery and makes a style statement. With this decorative function of wristwatches in mind, a wide range of materials has been used to create ornamental watch cases. Ladies watches have been particularly elaborately decorated.

Precious stones

Stones can be set in the case, dial, bezel or bracelet to turn an ordinary wristwatch into a dazzling piece of jewellery. All kinds of stones, semi-precious and precious, from marcasite to diamonds, have been used to adorn wristwatches.

Marcasite pieces from the 1920s and 1930s still exist in quantity. They occur mainly in the form of the slim, elegant lady's cocktail watches, often with straps made of velvet or satin ribbon or leather no thicker than a bootlace. Before buying one of these watches, it is important to check the condition of the movement. They were often inexpensive to start with and may not have survived in working order.

Where diamonds have been used, the quality of the setting and the colour of the gems are important if the watch is very heavily gem set, as in the case of any piece of jewellery. The type of cut used on the stones should also be examined to help value the watch and to date it. Where the diamonds are tiny, a simple eight-sided cut is understandable, but if the wristwatch has larger stones, they should be of good quality, colour and cut.

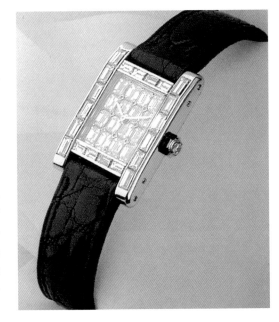

LEFT A simple leather strap carries an elaborate watch case in white gold set with diamonds so that none of the dial plate is visible.

BELOW An elaborate mans gold wristwatch from the 1960s. Produced in very limited numbers by Longines.

RIGHT Made in 1913, this white gold and diamond lady's strap watch by Cartier is an extremely important piece, due to the size of the stones above and below the watch case.

The case is not the only part of a watch's exterior that may be set with stones. The dials on both ladies' and men's watches can be made quite spectacular, with gemstones set in the positions of the numerals and dials made out of slabs of coloured stone or even rare woods, coral or mother-of-pearl, either plain or tinted. Gemstones may be used not only for the numerals, but also scattered all over the dial in a tight 'pave' formation, or at irregular intervals.

Design and designers

Why not alter the shape of a watch? Bangle watches, cuff watches and watches on bracelets all lend themselves to embellishment with gemstones, and the possible permutations are endless. The shape of the case may be heart-shaped, a half-circle or even a totally abstract non-geometric form.

The beauty of the jewellery watch is very often related to the thickness of the case and the way in which it may curve to follow the line of the wrist. Most examples of this kind of piece are fitted with a quartz movement and sapphire glass, but they cannot be made very water-resistant. Older pieces were often not water resistant, so it is important to treat this kind of watch with care. However, they will probably be strong enough for daily wear.

RIGHT A 14-carat gold Jaeger-Lecoultre from the 1950s.

The development of the extra-slim quartz movement in the mid-1970s made jewellery watches more accessible and opened out new design possibilities. Many new companies with fresh ideas were founded as a result; for some it was the start of a success story, whereas others with cheap and shoddy products were doomed to failure.

Raymond Weil

One of the successful companies was that of Raymond Weil. His Othello collection with an 18-carat gold electro-plated extra-slim case, with either a plain black dial or set with Austrian crystals, marked a new standard for middle-of-the-range jewellery pieces. The collection contained the slimmest quartz movement available in the price range and is well on the way to becoming a classic in its own right. It paved the way for Raymond

Weil's first solid gold and diamonds wristwatch, the Parsifal, carrying on the concept of elegance, which has been the company's trademark.

Although jewelled watches for men are present on the market, the most imaginative pieces are ladies', which include watches hidden inside bracelets, slim, elegant, pretty pieces, large, bold 'statements' and even sports watches made into items of jewellery.

Jean Lassale

Another relative newcomer to the jewellery watch scene is Jean Lassale. Since 1975, when the company laid claim to the slimmest watch in the world, it has received numerous prizes, awards and medals, but in 1985 it thrust itself forward with the Thalassa range. This featured highly-stylized watches with both ladies' and men's models.

The Jean Lassale Company decided that a watch must be not only functional, but also an object of beauty, giving true pleasure to the wearer. With ranges given such names as La Passion, it is not surprising that Jean Lassale watches have a unique appeal. A company whose early efforts included a watch called Mata Hari can, perhaps, only be expected

to continue with named models such as Scheherazade, and pieces which use lapis lazuli, diamonds, rubies and emeralds. The Stella model is a strap watch with an 18-carat gold accessory clip set with diamonds and rubies. Jean Lassale has also launched something of a novelty, a boxed set of two watches, 'his and hers', named the California range. This has a slightly more utilitarian look and feel, but carries over the unique Jean Lassale design and, with their water-resistant cases and straps, the watches are ideal for those who require strength and luxury.

ABOVE A pair of gold plated and crystal set watches from Raymond Weil.

ABOVE LEFT Stella, an elegant 18-carat gold and stone set watch by Jean Lassale, has a diamond and ruby accessory clip set.

LEFT Jennifer by Jean Lassale is set with diamonds and Lapis Lazuli.

RIGHT Three
watches with
turquoise,
malachite and
lapis lazuli
stone set dials
from Piaget.

The house of Piaget makes important jewellery pieces for both sexes. Its use of high-quality stones and the availability of the same piece with more or fewer gems allow a flexibility in the price range which makes it an excellent brand for the collector. This also applies to Baume et Mercier, which specializes in more delicate-looking jewellery pieces, including some beautifully crafted loose-link bracelets that are often attached to their watch cases with gem-set gold.

BELOW Baume
et Mercier made
this unusual
diamond
encrusted lady's
chronograph.

Jewellery watches can be innovative. For example, Jaeger-LeCoultre's Rendez-vous model has one of the wittiest, most whimsical concepts that you are likely to find in a lady's watch, with an outer rotating bezel set with a diamond which can be used discreetly to mark the time of a rendezvous. The Seductrice, one of Jaeger-LeCoultre's more recent models, demonstrates the versatility of precious stones. A curved watch case fits snugly on to a leather strap or a bracelet made of the same curves of precious gold.

Collecting

A jewellery watch need not be a major investment, but ensure that the movement is in good condition. Some people do wear old watches simply for their ornamental value. But for a good piece, it is worth making the effort to get the movement working. In a few cases, it may be possible to replace the movement completely.

Do not ignore the more traditional watch houses when searching for a jewellery piece. Rotary, Longines, Omega and Tissot all have produced jewellery ranges throughout the years. Ranges from the 1950s by Omega, with faceted crystals, are typical of their era. As early as 1930, Rotary produced some charming models using marcasite, some of them employing the concealed watch principle, which involved the piece of jewellery 'becoming' a watch at the flip of a catch.

CHAPTER SEVEN

COLLECTING CLASSICS

• • • •

A combination of factors makes a classic watch: durability of style and design and an understated elegance, plus strength of case and reliability of movement to withstand years of daily wear.

These qualities can be achieved only if manufacturers are prepared to spend time and trouble over their products. Unfortunately, it is not enough simply for a watch to wear well. Parts need to be available over the years, and straps must be found for strap watches if there is a special fitting involved. All this suggests some sort of continuity as far as the manufacturer is concerned. When you are buying a watch with such potential, remember that you will be wearing it for many years and its appearance must remain pleasing to you. In this regard, lasting style very often equals simplicity of design and purity of line; anything too fussy will probably not remain to your taste throughout the years to come.

LEFT An understated and elegant contemporary Vacheron Constantin.

RIGHT The Royal
Oak model by
Audemars Piguet
has been available
since the 1970s.

The great makers

Some watch houses have specialized more than others in the production of classic lines. They have been making the same basic designs for years, with perhaps only very slight variations in the dial or movement. These pieces have achieved their reputation through their performance over a long period of time, proving their strength, durability and refusal to cater for passing fads.

Blancpain, for example, despite huge pressure on the watch business as a whole since the 1970s, refuses to produce quartz movements and has, indeed, adopted as its maxim 'There has never been a quartz Blancpain and there never will be'. However, without going to such extremes, all reputable watch houses have a 'classic' line,

usually consisting of a strap watch with a plain gold case and either a white dial with black numerals or a champagne dial with baton markers, and available in versions for both men and women. These lines are generally manufactured for a number of years, discontinued, then reintroduced with slight variations to continue the original theme. It can be extremely interesting to locate the original of a particular range and follow it through to the present day.

If you can find them, old catalogues can be a valuable aid to building up this type of collection because they show the name of each range and list its various characteristics. A classic line does not mean an uninspired appearance. Sometimes the most innovative designs can prove to be enduring lines which can be developed over many years simply because the original concept was so good that no alteration was necessary to maintain its appeal.

Audemars Piguet

The Audemars Piguet watch factory was founded in 1875 by Jules Audemars and Edouard Piguet, yet another with its home in the Vallée de Joux in Switzerland where it was, at the time, the third largest employer – with ten employees! Today, descendants of the original founders are still directors of the company.

BELOW The Rado
company's early
Diastar model.

From its earliest years Audemars Piguet established itself as a manufacturer of complicated movements. In 1920 it was responsible for the smallest repeater watch, measuring only 16mm/⅝in in diameter.

In 1972, came the Royal Oak, named after three Royal Navy battleships. The design is of a quality that succeeds in emphasizing both simple and complicated movements, and its pinnacle was perhaps achieved with the automatic Quantième Perpétuel first produced in 1984 which is a much sought after major collector's item. The Royal Oak design sets off some of the most beautiful movements and lends itself to production in different metals, ranging from the traditional watchmaking materials to that relative newcomer to the industry, tantalum.

LEFT This wristwatch by Cartier looks as good now as it did when it was made in 1927.

stamp of craftsmanship, visible at a glance. Each order is the personal responsibility from beginning to end of an individual watchmaker, who signs the piece when it is finished. The Blancpain workshop, housed in a former farmhouse, is about as far from an assembly line as you can get.

Cartier

Since 1847, the name of Cartier has been synonymous with quality. The company is responsible for some of the most beautiful jewellery ever seen and has been translating its experience of incredibly high standards into the art of watchmaking since 1888. In the decades that followed, Cartier has produced countless pieces, each more beautiful than the last and, for many reasons, classic collectors' items in their own right.

BELOW A 1930s Santos by Cartier on a leather strap. Later versions usually have a metal bracelet.

Blancpain

When Jehan-Jacques Blancpain founded his watchmaking enterprise in the Jura Mountains in 1735, he established himself as a perfectionist. All Blancpain pieces still carry the undeniable

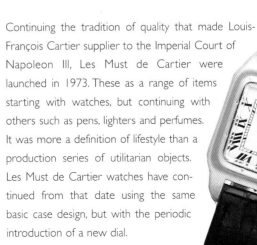

LEFT A contemporary Blancpain moonphase which shows the divisions of the lunar month.

Continuing the tradition of quality that made Louis-François Cartier supplier to the Imperial Court of Napoleon III, Les Must de Cartier were launched in 1973. These as a range of items starting with watches, but continuing with others such as pens, lighters and perfumes. It was more a definition of lifestyle than a production series of utilitarian objects. Les Must de Cartier watches have continued from that date using the same basic case design, but with the periodic introduction of a new dial.

ABOVE An elegant Dunhill contemporary classic.

The Cartier design team has shown, over the years, what can be done with a basic roman numeral dial, still maintaining the tradition of quality which makes Cartier such a great watchmaking name. For instance, the numerals can be enlarged so that they virtually join in the centre, or placed to run down the side of the case.

Dunhill

Not all watch brands that have enjoyed lasting popularity belong to a traditional watchmaking or jewellery firm. Alfred Dunhill, for example, that very English purveyor of luxury goods, has, since it was started at the beginning of the twentieth century, produced very fine pieces.

The most famous Dunhill wristwatch designs include the Vermeil (1975), the Millennium range (1982), the Elite (1986) and the Limited Edition Dress Watches.

Jaeger-LeCoultre

RIGHT A 1931 Reversos watch by Jaeger-LeCoultre. It has become one of the most famous classics.

When the first Monsieur LeCoultre settled in the Vallée de Joux during the sixteenth century, in the process of fleeing persecution by the Catholics in France, little did he realize that he was founding a dynasty. This was to come into its own in 1833 in a place called Le Sentier,

when Antoine LeCoultre opened his own watchmaking factory. Today, Jaeger-LeCoultre movements and cases are still produced by hand in Le Sentier.

The house of Jaeger-LeCoultre has been responsible for many 'firsts'. For example, in 1847, LeCoultre et Cie produced the first keyless watch mechanism, replacing the key with a crown winder on the side of the case.

Although not strictly to do with watchmaking, but of outstanding interest, the 'almost perpetual motion' Atmos Clock was also the brainchild of Jaeger-LeCoultre. This unique timepiece is powered by minute differences in temperature. Production has continued since 1930, and an example is traditionally presented to dignitaries by the Swiss government.

Another of the company's products has shown similar endurance – the Reverso, first produced in 1931 and still made. Combining the beauty and purity of line of the era of its conception with the strength necessary for the sportsman or sportswoman of that time, the Reverso, with its ability to pivot on itself to get out of harm's way, was a true classic in every sense right from the beginning.

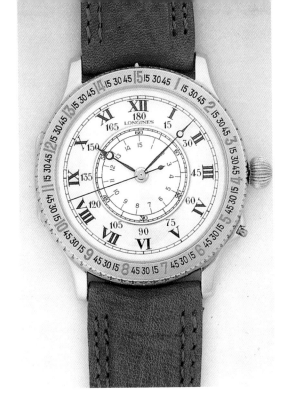

LEFT An 18-carat
gold watch from
the Lindbergh
range, designed by
Charles Lindbergh
himself.

Longines

The high quality watch making company Longines has also produced ranges of classic collectable wristwatches, perhaps the most interesting of its classics is the Lindbergh range which was designed and produced to commemorate the 1927 crossing of the Atlantic by Charles Lindbergh in his aeroplane, the *Spirit of Saint Louis*. This event gave birth to the idea of the Lindbergh collection in 1933 and indeed the original sketch for the wristwatch was made by Charles Lindbergh himself.

Another of the company's successes in durability, style and strength was the Conquest range, which although it is a very sports-orientated design, is slim and elegant enough to rate as a classic. The Conquest range is fitted with a quartz movement, which is revolutionary in that it could be guaranteed an accuracy of 12 seconds per year, an achievement even for quartz.

Omega

Omega has also produced a number of collectable ranges over the years, including not only the classic De Ville range, but also the more adventurously designed Constellation watch.

For the more experienced collector, Omega's Louis Brandt range, all automatic, comprises a perpetual calendar, a chronograph and a plain automatic movement in 18-carat gold on leather straps. This range was produced to celebrate the company's founder, Louis Brandt (1825–1879).

BELOW A hand-
wound Omega
from 1967, part of
the De Ville range.

RIGHT The gold
Rolex Oyster from
1927 was one of
the first
waterproof
watches.

Rolex, did
not confine itself
to the production of sports or
sports-orientated watches. In 1931,
a patent was granted for the Perpetual mechanism, thanks to which, in 1945, the Rolex Datejust
became the first wristwatch with a date display on the
watch face. Again, taking the idea further proved to be
no problem for the Rolex company, and in 1956, the
Day-Date was launched.

Rolex

Hans Wilsdorf, a name remembered by all watch lovers,
was the founder of the Rolex watch company in 1905.
By 1910, Rolex had obtained the first
chronometer certificate ever awarded to
a wristwatch. The firm worked hard to
improve the strength of wristwatches,
which were, at that time, prone to dam-
age by dust and humidity.

By 1926, it was conducting tests
which involved immersing a watch
in water for three weeks, and in
1927, Mercedes Glietze swam
the English Channel wearing a
Rolex Oyster. The company had
found the solution to the problem of making a watertight case
with the invention of the screw-
down crown in what was, for Rolex,
the beginning of a series of watches,
each guaranteeing water resistance to
unheard-of depths.

It is uncertain which Rolex model is the
most collectable, from the earliest cushion
shapes to the well-known Datejust. For
many, Rolex pieces represent the climax of
the art of watchmaking and, even for the
non-connoisseur, their image is one of
the ultimate in luxury and desirability.

This chapter has discussed the
work of only a very small number of the watch houses which
produce classic pieces whose
fame and collectability has
remained constant throughout
the years. There are many more,
not all of which have achieved such
international recognition, but which
are worth searching for on account of
their quality, even if a little tenacity is
required to locate a particular model.

RIGHT A Rolex
Perpetual Datejust
in steel and yellow
metal with
sapphire glass and
a screw down
crown.

SWATCH

● ● ● ●

In the late 1970s Swiss watchmaking was sinking deeper into recession. On an international level the economy was looking good, so there was a potential market for watches. Nonetheless, the Swiss industry was suffering frequent closures and redundancies. The Japanese, meanwhile, had eased their way into quartz movement production and were constantly occupied in perfecting their skills and refining their products.

Two important Swiss watch groups were affected by this growing crisis. Allgemeine Schweizerische Uhrenindustrie AG (ASUAG) and Société Suisse pour l'Industrie Horlogère (SSIH) – now combined as the Swiss Corporation for Microelectronics and Watchmaking Industries Ltd (SMH) – put their heads together and, spurred on by imminent disaster, came up with an extra-flat movement only 1.98mm (²⁄₂₅in) thick. Called the Delirium, its production and development led the way to a simpler quartz movement costing much less than was previously feasible.

The new movement was ideal for a project in hand, which called for a movement as inexpensive as possible to fit into a plastic case. The final producer of the watch (it was not initially intended to be sold as an 'own label')

would need only to specify the colour required. After the number of pieces normally used in a quartz movement had been reduced from 91 to 51 and experiments had been carried out with items such as Lego building blocks and disposable cigarette lighters for the moulding of the case, Swatch was ready to be born. It had taken three years of intensive planning to produce a waterproof, shock-resistant accurate watch made of synthetic materials with a low production cost.

BELOW Tadanori Yokoo (GZ107, Rorrim 5), Swatch Art, 1987.

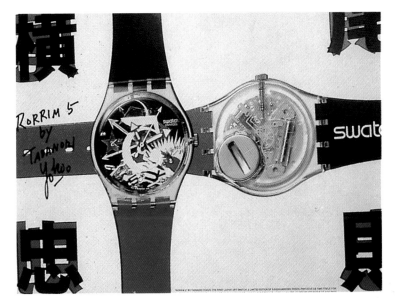

RIGHT Yuri
(GG118), Igorts
Swatch, 1992.

It was decided that the new product would be marketed in-house. It was not enough simply to produce such a watch; the idea of a quality item made of synthetic material had to be communicated to the public. A catchy, easily recognizable name had to be found. A New York advertising executive came up with the winning idea. The promotional slogan for the launch was to have been: 'You have a second home, why not a second watch?', which resulted in S-Watch, and finally, by 1981, the name Swatch.

Design and innovation

The first Swatches were released to the public on 1 March, 1983. There were 12 models and a maximum selling price of SWfr49.90. The launch was carried out in Switzerland, Germany and Great Britain. That year also saw the initial planning and conception of the Pop Swatch. From a simple idea sprang one of the most innovative design concepts of our time. Swatch watches are highly collectable. It is ideal for the beginner, because of its huge following (there are collectors' clubs in most countries) and its reasonable price.

RIGHT 700 years
Swiss Confederacy,
Flack (GZ117) by
Niklaus Troxler,
Swatch Art, 1991.

FAR RIGHT
Swatch
Chronograph
Signal flag
(SCN 101).

From the spring of 1984, all Swatches produced were given a name as well as a number. With the first Swatch Specials, the collecting of Swatches may be said to have truly begun. The first Special was the original Jelly Fish (1983), which was closely followed by the 1984 Olympic Specials.

One of the most remarkable Specials was the Puff series, which had as its theme, the slogan 'Blow your time away'. This was the 1988 Christmas Special. Christmas Specials began in 1987 with the GZ 105, Bergsträssli, followed by the Christmas 1988 Bonaparte, but these were mere preliminaries leading up to Christmas 1992 and the Chandelier.

As an indication of Swatch's popularity, when a shop was set up in London's Covent Garden for one day and allocated 1,000 pieces, enthusiasts from all over the world formed a queue and by 4pm that day the shop had sold out.

Christmas Specials are one facet of the Swatch story. There are also Swatch Chronographs, Scuba Swatches, Maxi Swatches, Art Swatches, Swatch Automatics, the Swatch Pager and lately the 'Swatch Musicall', a musical alarm Swatch designed by Jean Michel Jarre.

More than meets the eye

From the start, Swatch proved that it was much more than just a frivolous fun watch. It showed that Swiss technology and expertise could be used for something visually exciting to all age groups, which would also be inwardly as reliable and as sturdy as one of the heaviest stainless-steel sports watches.

Swatch decided to put itself to the test and produced a run of 4,843 Swatches which were issued with chronometer certificates. These pieces were submitted to an amazing range of tests, including freezing temperatures, 90-degree humidity and, not least, being left for 24 hours on a vibration machine. Obviously, with an issue of only 4,843 pieces worldwide, Swatch Chronometers do not often appear on the market, but their very existence is proof, if it were needed, of the company's commitment to maintaining quality regardless of price.

Thinking big

Swatch 'sees big' with a Swatch measuring 2m 10cm (6ft 6¾in). It is designed to be hung on a wall in the home or office, and is really a piece of furniture. The company went further still with the largest Swatch ever made — it weighs 13 tonnes and is 167m (548ft) long.

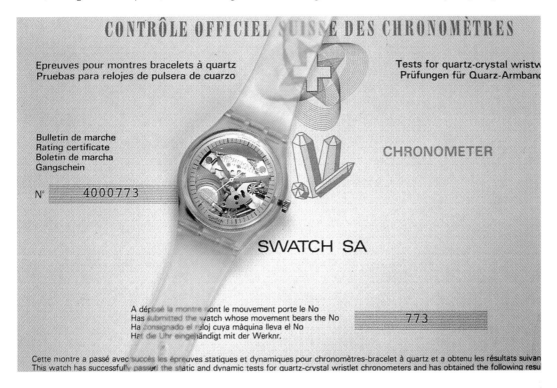

LEFT Jelly fish chronometer (GK 100) with a certificate, 1990.

RIGHT Watches
in the 'One More
Time' series were
made to look
like food.

Popular Swatch

The Pop Swatch is an outsize watch that pops off its strap, which is also very large. This is yet another success story, both in its ordinary form and as one of the Pop Swatch Art series or Christmas Specials. The strap was designed to fit over the sleeve of an overall, an idea from the old aviator watches. A further development in this model is the mid-sized version, larger than an ordinary Swatch, but smaller than a standard Pop Swatch.

LEFT Swatch Chronograph, Sandstorm
SCB 104, 1990/91

RIGHT Swatch Chronograph Skipper
SCN 100, 1990/91

Mechanical Swatch

Although Swatch was launched as the ultimate in simplified quartz movements, when a renewed interest in mechanical movements became apparent, the company brought out its automatic wristwatch. First available in 1991, it is both shock- and water-resistant. The mechanical Time to Move model bears the logo of the Earth Summit held in Rio de Janeiro in 1992.

Crowd stoppers

1990 saw the arrival of the Swatch Chronograph, a sophisticated movement with four stepping motors, yet the case is the same size as an ordinary Swatch. The Swatch Chronograph has functions to record finishing time and intermediate time and a tachometer for speed indication. Early chronographs are much sought after.

The company has gone further with the Stop Swatch: the first push on the button sends the hands back to twelve o'clock and another push starts a stop watch with a six-hour range.

Capable of withstanding depths of up to 200m (650ft), the Swatch Scuba has a timing bezel with brightly coloured, clear numerals. The models have mainly nautical names, such as Captain Nemo and Sea Grapes.

Pager/Piepser

One of the latest brainchildren of the Swatch engineers, is the world's first wristwatch with a built-in radio receiver. Its electronics necessitate 120 square metres (1,290 square feet) of silicon, compared with 3.5 square metres (38 square feet) in an ordinary Swatch. An antenna under the crystal picks up signals from one of four pre-determined callers. The next generation will be able to show the number of the caller.

Collecting Swatches

The permutations for collecting Swatches are clearly endless. Not only has the company produced limited editions, special and singles, but there is also a whole series by major contemporary artists: for instance, the Pop Swatch Art Series, One More Time, by Alfred Hofkunst, which comprises three models.

The firm's first art watch, which has recently been sold at auction for a very large sum of money, was the 1985 Kiki Picasso. This was followed in 1986 by a series by Keith Haring featuring four pieces.

LEFT Swatch Chronograph: Skate Bike SCB 105, 1990/91.

LEFT SDK 100 deep blue SDN 400 Bora Bora and the Swatch Scuba 200, 1990/91.

63

RIGHT Christmas in Vienna: Mozart (GZ 114), 1989.

The year 1987 was represented by the Folon Series, together with Tadanori Yokoo. In 1988, there was the Foundation Maeght Series by artists, such as Pol Bury, Valerio Adami and Pierre Alechinsky. The Mimmo Paladino 1989 Art Swatch has been quoted as selling for up to US$25,000.

Getting started

BELOW Christmas: Hollywood dream (GX 116), Swatch Specials, 1990.

However, before embarking on a search for such elusive pieces, it may be more practical to set your sights a little lower and concentrate on some of the early singles. If you decide to become a Swatch collector, you will be joining a worldwide club with over 130,000 members. Its own newspaper, *The Swatch Journal*, aims to transmit information to club members as speedily as possible. Club members are offered special Swatches available only to them and not sold through normal outlets. The company also makes available to members a yearly catalogue to bring them up to date on the four annual launches: spring, summer, autumn and winter.

An unforseen success

The Swatch creators did not set out to start a trend, but Swatch mania has prevailed since the early days, and each new product launched has been greeted with such enthusiasm that, in some cases, supply has been far outstripped by demand. The reasons behind all this are simple enough – Swatch has

an excellent product selling for the right price and a marketing team capable of taking it into realms not thought of by anyone else. Moreover, the watch's bright colours and affordability appeal to younger people, its reliability attracts the purist, who wants a highly precise timekeeper, and the sportsperson is also catered for with the chronographs and diving watches.

Finally, because Swatch's popularity has snowballed – even in the art world. thanks to the Art Specials – there are now models kept in glass cases in museums which, for a watch which started out as an inexpensive 'second watch', is truly an achievement.